ALL THAT COMES TO LIGHT

ALL THAT COMES TO LIGHT

Poems by
Lisa Malinowski Steinman

Arrowood Books
Corvallis, Oregon

Versions of these poems first appeared in *Threepenny Review, Spoon River Review, Boulevard, Willow Springs, Aileron, Colorado Review, Calapooya Collage, Ironwood, Visions, Another Chicago Magazine, Prism International, Tendril, Webster Review, MSS, Rhapsody, Penny Dreadful, Epoch, The Chicago Review, The Gritloaf Anthology, Encore, Dekalb Literary Journal, and Apple*.

The writing of this book was made possible in part through support from the Oregon Arts Commission and the National Endowment for the Arts.

Typeset at Arrowood Books and Corvallis Typesetting, Inc.
Printed by Cascade Printing, Corvallis, Oregon.

Arrowood Books, Inc., P.O. Box 2100, Corvallis, OR 97339

Library of Congress Cataloging-in-Publication Data

Steinman, Lisa Malinowski, 1950 -
All that comes to light: poems / by Lisa Steinman.

ISBN 0-934847-10-X (alk. paper).
ISBN 0-934847-11-8 (pbk.: alk. paper).

I. Title.

PS3569.T3793A78 1989
811′.54—dc19

For Zenon and Shirley Malinowski

"To explain grace requires a curious hand."
—Marianne Moore

Contents

1. LANGUAGE WITHOUT GEOGRAPHY

2. NIGHTWORK

3. FAMILIARITY

1. LANGUAGE WITHOUT GEOGRAPHY

THE DIFFICULTY OF TRANSLATION [illegible]
[illegible] THE ANGST OF MOVING

ON THE NEED FOR TEACHERS

I am losing poems again these days;
the ones that get away could change our lives.
Proust told us about the madeleine, but who will explain the smell of
tomatoes?
Green, it fills and arranges the world.
Everything falls into place, brightens and flies right.

These plants open an empty world; they feed on nothing—
there are no green tomatoes in my past:
my father's garden was dark and sad among the pine trees and the weeds.
There is a woman in a jump suit next to me, reading a journal.
She has just underlined in yellow pen:
for teachers, imagination is important.
She will try to memorize this fact and miss the boat.

I have inner voices that sing to me, saying
"You have no inner voice." We have an argument on this.
It's like being all wing and no bird in sight.

My grandfather, poor poet, was published—his great pride—
in the *Congressional Record*. It was a filibuster.
I carry on: poems, all filibuster, avoiding the point.

Six years after I left home, in a diner, I saw a woman I had disliked.
She was not happy, and I walked by
as if I were invisible, or memory an imagined thing.
This I would forgive myself, if I could.

We all die, and if the good first, then not so good.
My grandfather lives only in my memory of his pleasure
in poems and thick, white bread.
My mother and father—smaller at each visit—
no longer hold the world at bay.
I wish I could love the educator in the jump suit:
imagination fails at every turn.

ACCENTS

> "Suppose the eye were an animal. Then seeing would be
> its soul. The blind eye is not an eye, except only in name."
> —Aristotle

> "The tongue is an eye."
> —Wallace Stevens

The sun and the city turn an unnatural pink;
palm trees stud the horizon like sequins, and cars tumble down the freeway.
You sit in your too-long, baby-blue parka at the kitchen table,
weighing less and less, a gymnast defying gravity.

We into the secrets of beer and making lists
of post office and grocery runs,
avoiding your lightness that marks an allergy we share to
earth, city, home.

That traitor, my tongue, in what it will not say names over and over
the cold your parka will not stop.
The stories of what you've seen today rush through your laugh
that begins, also, where your life is making raids on silence.

Who will show us how to live well?
The eye creeps off into its lair, refusing food.
The tongue attempts an architecture, evolving a city for the eye.
The streets fill slowly with speech:

a man near the repair shop chatting up an empty car,
a boy riding his bicycle fast down the road,
a third wheel on the handlebars,
talking loudly to the world his pedaling blurs.

MEDITATIVE FUGUE

Ecstasy: from the Greek, *ek*— (out) and *histanai* (to place)

The couple at the next table is clearly in trouble,
discussing geography and love.
They are like dinosaurs, requiring conditions
that could be detailed with great exactness.
Too much ice, for instance, and it's all over.

The same might be said of desire in other guises,
where you'd thing exactness wasn't needed.
As when Yogi Berra thanked his friends at an award dinner
"for making this evening necessary."
Or consider: enough monkeys could type *Paradise Lost*.

This is false; the monkeys need someone to order their words.
She says, "While there should be evenings when anything is possible,
keeping one foot on the ground makes ecstasy difficult."
He wants more than the world;
what is necessary is less.

Scientists are asking how to get stuff from particles
and what makes stars work.
We dine under the same stars, on an earth full of road signs—
"rocks," "wind gusts": we will know just what hit us.
The working of stars is not enough for my couple.

He says, "Extinction is not a sign of failure."
She wants to know of what, then, it is a sign, and how she is to take it.
As with other signs reading "no *right* turn,"
or dinosaurs browsing through the Jurassic,
we all feel slightly out of place.

A SHARP MIND CONTEMPLATES THE COMFORTS OF THE SUN

The flora has outdone itself:
banana flowers, like reptilian birds, brood
over the landscape.
Grotesqueries of fruit hang everywhere.

Cars gestate for twenty years here,
tend to eat their young;
rubber spatulas reproduce like rabbits, and flap at our heels.
A sprawling Afghan,
found in a room from which two lovers disappeared last week,
is being held for questioning.
The coverlet is gaudy, sullen, close-knit.

An embarrassment of creatures loiter in the warmth;
an overblown capybara noses the air;
off-shore, a manatee soaks up the comforts of the sun.
Nothing is left to desire. And daily,

the sun, she rise, plotting a line sharp enough
to cut through all this generosity.

LANDSCAPES, FAMILIES, AND LOSS

—after a painting by John Martin, 1932

Our language and our cities evict us.
It's like planting bulbs, spider-like roots scrambling for dark.
"Dig in," I tell myself, and then,
"Dig out." The problem is: do we want the earth or not.

Last night we watched the Hunter's moon,
low as a street light in the park, shadows webbing out in all directions.
Old songs about young love came back to us in pieces,
and each time we stepped between two trees we faced a whole new world.

Today the clouds race by, stopping for nothing.
It's fall: air, birds, leaves crisp
in the barrenness of things.
What is it that we can't rest here?

I want to settle the language and landscapes into which we curl ourselves,
the memories of home that ensnare us like the moon.
I mistrust the moonlight, but also call out, "Change me,"
though I must confess it never does.

There is still a woman in the grocery store who complains about her feet
to the line snagged on a box of something no one's ever bought before;
at the bus stop, a boy full of vitamins and Jung;
a portly grandfather in Ryan's Lunch.

The formica does not please him as he sits over coffee and the *Times*.
In 1932, the city was decorous. The strange fruit of the sun sank
between grey forms and composed windows through which the light
declined.
The geometry was everything, and just about right.

We all do day labor now, and the bars all serve us beer.
The dark lines of phone wires spread out from the roof pitches
like a sunset within which the sun rests like a pigeon in an empty house.
Whatever we are waiting for, we do not like the wait.

The day's blank stretches out like an old man on a park bench,
covered with the daily news.

LAYING CLAIM TO THE HEIGHTS

—Yosemite, California

Hard to set one's self by the seasons here—
understory plants flirt with the sun;
the rest thin out in sparse air.
Even this much detail's hard to come by.
A few odd, off-balance creatures skitter in the trees.
Three climbers scale the higher peaks.

Flying out, the waves seemed frozen in place—
a corrugated solid, hard to tell from the clouds.
Our descent into a storm front, like entering a forest fire;
the wing-tip light, a distant city.

I used to fly.
Did it well, though slow, and two feet off the ground.
Even leaping from promontories, there'd be this graceless sinking until
my feet scraped every fallen log.
It would be easier to walk.

You await me at every landing—
compact, prickly, not sure you want to be here.
I tell you squirrels eat the acorns now the Indians are gone;
and Jeffrey pine should smell just so:
fruity,
overripe.

The men appear as dots, fall
into our waiting eyes.
I point them out, "climbers,"
and they leave the words behind like spikes.

LANDGODS ARE NOT EASILY TRANSPORTABLE

The landscape provides anticipation.
We know just enough not to question,
knowing too, in this belated day,
not to stand around expectant.
Can one say,
"I'm waiting for an extraordinary sky,
preferably not too disastrous"?

There's a bad rate of exchange;
the economy of grace is unstable.
Our charms no longer work,
or sit ill with middle age.
Who's still charmed by the thrust and parry of wit,
after which we've named a wrestle-hold for the drowning?

Mere cadences sustain us, then,
as when children who cannot speak intone
with the seriousness of lecturers lecturing

on how our resources peter out,
and no more building is allowed,
and how there remains a flirtation with sense,
and glimpses of rock and night.

The moon tonight:
as if one corner of the sky has been erased with a #2 pencil,
badly.

INHERITING THE EARTH

I am flying to my sister, whose husband was just killed.
He asked a neighbor to turn down the stereo.
I never did like flying,
but this coming back to earth is no great shakes.

The airport is full of causes.
There are people who want to end the world:
a sweet white-haired woman lobbies for capital punishment.
The neighbor didn't have to shoot him.

My sister is surrounded by vast emptinesses that go on forever.
This is the world of the living.
The mourners tiptoe around her, sizing up the estate:
four records, a pair of drums, many pieces of worn-out clothing

and dreams. This is the inheritance of the poor,
over which they will fight.
My sister moves as if she is afraid she will shatter
the silence around her.
Other neighbors are still playing their music very loud.

PLANTING FISH

There are moments when we inhabit the world
as when the air is heavy with mist clutching the field,
or it's about to rain,
or just has.

I used to think this had something to do with love
or desire:
whatever I turned to withered and died, but behind me whole gardens
appeared.
The trees would gather in the upper left hand corner of the field for days.

I would notice,
my noticing a charm to ward them off.
Meanwhile, the dogwood would bloom—
first time in twenty years.
I'd expect as much, take credit for a kind of sharecropping.

But this is not right.
Behind my back, a tree fingers a lamp post like a kid making the sign
of a cuckold over his sister for the family album,
not knowing what that Indian dress,
two feathers over the head,
might mean.
The tree's sign is not like planting fish with corn,
a generous exchange of goods.
I think rather it suggests we are not at home here, and, more,
do not know what we lack.
Not the world.
The philosophical tree rises, incurable monster:
terrible,
perhaps true,
and no help at all.

DRIVING TO BUFFALO

Junked cars, patched snow—this human arrangement
with clutter used to please me; now decay insists
upon itself. My father tells me he reads less,
no longer waits for something to change
his life. The landscape agrees: what persists
confers on us no blessing.

I read. Columbus storms the library;
his picture's hung. The library takes the figure with flagrant
disrespect . . . so stiff it seems the flag is planting him. We smile.
I'm reading *Newsweek*, *Time*, which say
cuisine enters with us an age of less—no fat, but "very elegant."
We can, at least, lose heart with style.

This is an argument on more
or less. My father may be right; there's nothing we can use.
There's nothing more to say.
Bare facts: things die; we're killing people in El Salvador.
Garage sales pass unwanted goods around. I look for something
—hardly news,
and not so much to change my life as to resist defeat.

A POEM THAT ENDS UP LOOKING LIKE BRAZIL

"It is human nature to stand in the middle of a thing,
but you cannot stand in the middle of this."
—Marianne Moore

I'm reading of America's yen for poems containing history.
Meanwhile carpenter ants do a high wire act on the phone lines to the
house,
vandals turning basements into lacey remnants.

It's hard to stand firm in the middle, says Ez.
I'm woolgathering;
ideas wander off like naked sheep.
Poems containing history, boas bulging with mice, are slow to digest.
If sod were air, we could thread our way through
these roots from below, disrupting termites, old tin cans,
clinging to the underbelly of the land;
just so Odysseus escaped Cyclops. Back home
Penelope scuttles her craft.

Children hoot outside my window.
I'm a mean old bat, rejecting noise.
The innocent eyes sees nothing. We see what tradition lets us see,
patchworks of all we've read. We don't work at history;
it works us—refreshing and wicked and real.

Just now in Tunis they've mild lions and fierce snails,
small things that bite, out of control.
Galileo put Tunis right off the map; he set the Sorbonne on its ear.
Things creep into my poems uninvited;
like making a discovery or a new friend,
this makes me feel woven into some fabric with the microscopic,
barnacles, and ants
unsettling all the foundations.

2. NIGHTWORK

THE CROSSING

There is a buoyancy the sun provides,
by which we know that something is about to happen.
Light fantails over the hills,
preys on everything. Being restless,
we set out to track down all these promises.

Something is about to happen—
we hear the flap and glide of hawks,
circling, closing in.
We must make light of ourselves to follow;
cross rivers as if on turtles that crack or scatter
as we give each carapace our full weight.

Here a pine tree, washed in jottings, glows
a deeper green at center.
It grows from the edges inward.
Behind us, a burning alphabet dreams of milkweed, geese, and terrapin,
of all that comes to light.

WE PASS THROUGH THE NIGHT TO THE KINGDOM OF HEAVEN

1. *The Kingdom of Heaven in the Mind's Eye*

Angels go picking elephants up like daisies.
Elephants pick angels up and drink them down.
We watch breathless, pale, amazed.
Otherwise,
things go on as usual.

Except we have all these elephants left hanging around.
How many angels to nourish an elephant?
These days, we can't afford angels:
as difficult to find as a needle in a haymow.

2. *The Celebration of a Day*

Angels, my eye.
Elephants,
in a pig's eye.
A day like a pineapple.
Even the cars display grace:
a blue pickup
stitches the dump road to the idiot sun.

And at night we design
the full moon through storm clouds,
in the eye of the storm;
a night like a pearl; a pause; the night
a period at the end of the day's sentence.

RUMINATIONS

> "At most a few superfluous recollections may succeed
> in smuggling themselves through the half open door."
> —Bergson

It's Halloween.
The children come as their own nightmares.

Our cow has just calved.
Two legs first appear on the floor.
A perfect bullcalf named Stanley stands in the barn.
In time he'll become a yearling whom we'll eat,
chewing the unexpected meat slowly.

On a Greyhound bus once I met a girl
who lived only to eat.
"My friends they need money for anything and I got it,
it's theirs;
my clothes they can have anytime.
But any son of a bitch so much as looks at my food . . ."
she said,
eating her way to New York City.
Returning from the dentist the week before
full of novocaine
she had thoughtfully consumed half of her lower lip
along with a roast beef sandwich.
My daughter walks the streets dreaming of knifing people.

* * *

I should be asleep but this silence fills with gossip or daily chores.
I can hear street noises outside.
Trying to count sheep, I conjure a fence,
attempt to stand it still in a reasonable plane.
Kangaroos bound over it.
I had counted on sheep.
These other creatures rushing the gate keep me awake.

NIGHTWORK:
WHO WILL SAVE US FROM WILLIMANTIC, CONNECTICUT?

I often return there at night.
A dingy film lays claim to whoever enters.
Bright clothing immediately turns garish.
Woolworth's makes everything its own.

It's all so clear:
the crabgrass and pitted green railings embedded in the sidewalks;
three concrete steps to each front porch;
landmarks:
"The Site of the First Silkmill in America!"
The mill itself, long since removed to Dearborn Village, Michigan.

Young boys prowl the streets for love,
and each night I prowl with them,
eagerly divesting dirty-haired young girls of their bright dresses,
before the alarm leaves me exhausted,
dissipated.
There are so few of us nightworkers left
to save the children of Willimantic.

LISTENING TO THE DUCKS

The universe expands to its natural limit,
testing that last quarter inch beyond which nothing yields.
The world curls into its appointed space,
comes to rest with faint twitchings.
Or so they say.
And one day, at four, perhaps,
one Tuesday afternoon as we pick our way down the coast before going
home,
the world will snap back, elastic, to a single point.
Bones will be gathered from the four corners, ready to be restrung,
quivering at the jolt.

The winds will beat us to the top of the mountain,
while we attend the slower rise of trees and sea converging;
note mussels still clinging to rocks with long and tacky threads of
themselves;
and ducks flinging their voices out over the water,
bodies trailing.

The furnace spends the night lumbering back and forth across the basement.
Unsettled, we call out our bearings; know
what we take on faith will not keep, but shudder,
kneel down under all that holds us to ourselves.
Meanwhile we still find comfort in small likenesses;
dance and caper on the unpaved road.

FOOLISH GRACE, SEDUCED BY WIT

We show ourselves, knowing word gets back.
Probably just that old, slow, winding toward desire—
the one faithful timepiece all our own.
We keep each other longing for a quick sweep, clean as a whistle;
search for a sterner watch, to put us in our place.
        There at last, one would come to play us silly
        until we yelp with abandoned pleasures:
        cluttered woods and '52 DeSoto;
        winter wheat tinged orange;
        spiders courting the air.
This point-to-point returns a little less convincing,
scope narrowed, each time.
We keep our stranglehold on the difficult transition between glut
and will; pay sweet attentions to ourselves; tone down.
The weather swells with distant announcers, speaking without tongues.

No special pleading here, no speech direct.
We sprint for ever smaller stakes,
lest we burst through like thoroughbreds who ditch their riders,
cross the finish wire ahead of the first jockey.
Takes the edge off winning.
Nothing is created or destroyed,
but much is lost.

FOOLISH GRACE DEFINES HER HERO WITH MALICE; LEAVES HIM HIGH AND DRY

"the question is, which is to be master?"

You bury people casually,
hold your own except in brief and puzzling moments:
anything is possible here.
I want to be told what will befall me,
and then watch the fall.
Think I don't allow you your possession,
needing you solid, wise, perverse?
Though I envy your long string of capable women,
I want only what does not want me;
gave you title to what I wanting so hard made.

And once possessing,
found it difficult to distinguish vigor from malice:
this brawl in which you put your foot down,
get the upper hand.
Bestows off-balance like some seesaw
not to leave us settled in the air.

You upped the stakes,
but my intemperance keeps you in control:
I won't let you down.
Like to draw a plumb-line from your high cravings,
leave you, compose myself,
and find my shadow grown too big for your britches.

KEEPING PIGEONS: FOOLISH GRACE COMPOSES A POEM TO THE MUSE

It bothers me that my curses return.
They are, like pigeons, banded:
complaints saved up for years.
I have raised this flock especially for you.
Born and bred in your actions, they have no loyalty.

Traitors, they betray my charge.
I keep to my revenge,
train my grievances with care,
taking them a little further from home each day,
plotting that you will find yourself accused by these returning missiles.

Look, I am sending you your life.
I return your image,
tired of remaking myself.
(The birds march from their eggs month after month:
all unfailingly pigeons.)
Beware.
You might find yourself planing through these pages.
These are your gestures; this inconstancy, yours.

I bring home your fowl,
bind evil messages to their faithless feet, and turn them loose
to find you. Instead,
they settle down and make themselves comfortable:
fat, unnatural aviators come home to roost.

FOOLISH GRACE GETS AMBITIOUS; LECTURES THE MOON

"for all intents and purposes"

Ridiculous to set our sights so high.
All these high-flown phrases,
navigators feathering caps and nests,
although we should know where you begin to pale.
We'd think our credit good,
settle for our place in the sun, to bleach dry,
still this fidgeting.

Knowing more your pull, each cell straining for the sky.
You spark that old come-hither, and we quiver and thrill.
Defying you, just like fending off the sea.
These tides dally with us
                                        as with anemones,
brown fists closing over whatever flirts by,
indeterminate creatures for all our slow consuming.
Waves edge upon the shore like nervous fingers;
on the bald rocks, gulls place and replace each other like fleas.

Let others cure themselves: we land on sheer precipice,
require constantly to keep the air below.
All night we crest, dreaming floods and swells, objects out of place.

The sands bristle with ribs, strayed bones,
rich with the shock of what's gone wrong.
        Those sailors—what plans they laid
        to avoid the rough bargain of land and sea clinched over them.

WAXING ELOQUENT AND CASTING PEARLS

Tonight, as I drive you to your new home, my love,
there is a flat purple oyster of a cloud under the moon.
For a moment, this fortuitous blotch of moonlight and pollution
lightens our mood.

A moon on the half shell is served
because I have listened to you tell me your fears.
You spin your tale well, insinuating yourself,
although I am the one harmed,
and you with the gall to ask sympathy for your loss of yourself
as a good man.

I know our wit slowly covers a multitude of sins,
casts up a pearly moon from the poisonous sky.
This time, I bequeath you *my* moon:
knit of wholecloth, a trick of lighting.
Men have walked upon the moon:
it's all dust and empty
and very cold.

SAYING GOOD-BY TO CARY GRANT

I cry at old movies but never admit this to anyone,
knowing no Mack trucks really do appear on the horizon
to dispose of villians cleanly.
No villians, for that matter,
appear to be available.

Having held you once at arm's length,
I seem to have established a certain distance between us.
I can't say how much I regret this.
I suspect you admire me precisely as one who keeps her distance.
That's fine.
It's you and I and all this empty space.
The script writers have gone home.

On this page, there's no clear sailing:
we navigate the shallows triumphantly,
and realize we've lost the map.
No stellar performances here.
Cary Grant gets his girl and sails into the sunset.
We go home, do the vacuuming, and pay the rent—
always on time.

THE DOVE RETURNS, BEDRAGGLED AND WITH SOMETHING TO SAY

Okay,
so you didn't like the berries.
Listen,
back then we were all nervous,
got used to it,
came to like that aura of eerie exaltation.
We were on edge, which made it easy to find salvage special:
the myrtle, the juniper, moose droppings, the dribs and drabs.
And then after a while

we missed the whitecaps and treachery.
We're all in the same boat now.

You think it's fun being just another pigeon in the dovecoat?
I hate this jigsaw puzzle done by an expert shut-in, a piece missing
where the corner of the clapboard house eats into the sky . . .
no carcass, no buzzard, nothing that sticks to the ribs.

When the ice came this time, we laid in stores at first,
straining to hear a bird exercise its voice;
thoughts slid off the landscape, though it didn't look dangerous:
the Douglas fir stiff outside the drapes like an oversized peeping Tom.

We said
this winter still-life pleases—
a posture copied from a pleasure we recalled anticipating.
Yet we woke uprooted from dreams:
the ice would deepen.

In sleep, when we opened the door, seals of ice shattered.
The shrubbery bore clear, globe-like fruit; each blade of grass,
a skeleton inside a rounded skin.
Birds landed on branches, glancing off, startled.

We picked our way through the strange cavernous harvest,
straightening at each step like birches throwing off a frozen weight,
to stand,
scattered bars of off-white.

But now we know spring will come again.
This time I bring a problem: how not to imagine disaster,
to have no fascination with the curiosities left scarred
and oddly angled from the storm.

AN ANATOMY OF DREAMS

"Join hands as we may, one of the hands is mine
and the other is yours."
—Stanley Cavell

You say when I wake you, "I'm busy carrying bridges across rivers."
The night before, I asked where all the green birds had gone.
Band tailed pigeons moved into the larch.
Then, in the gathering cold,
even they left.
Obviously, we both have our work cut out for us.

Some days I think we should be more like Greeks
decked out in white togas among white buildings
thinking lofty geometrical thoughts,
clear bright lights shining in intercranial space.
I worry our lives close down
the way homeowners cordon off upper floor guest rooms
to save on heating bills.

Next door, our neighbor dreams of her children grown,
the pantry full of canned goods (not too exactly labelled).
The laundry is done.
Her days flow, a gentle current in black and fresh, clean white.

I don't know this is bad.
In heaven, the laundry will always be done.
There will be a poetry of Boraxo or Cheer,
and we'll practice the blessedness of shopping carts.

Most of us were born on Saturdays—
no beauty, no grace, not so giving. We work hard.
That's a *real* bird we say on Thanksgiving,
by which we do not mean our turkeys teeter
between existence and non-being,
but that we eat and it is good.

Living as we do, we dream of birds and bridges.
I can't help thinking what they figure we will one day have;
they are anchored on the earth.
And I remember my father, who loved opera, singing me to sleep on trips.
I know the music hidden in all the highway signs from Ann Arbor to Boston.
For me, the highest moments still come in the most mundane language:
Exit. Emergency Parking. Food. Gas. Lodging.

At night, in my house now, flocks of birds fly the coop,
arcing up to fill the sky over your pile of bridges.
We both have our hands too full, as we pause, to wave good-by.

THE DIFFICULTY OF TRANSLATION IN THE MIDST OF MOVING

Rain hangs over our city like a thick, black bar.
On days like this, we turn to our friends, for company,
translating the weather into shared beer, small talk and gain.
Sam tells me *translation* comes from the Latin
for across, within, between, beyond, over, above or through,
and has also to do with *latera*, lungs, the burden of the air
as it moves across, within, between (and so on)
our bodies. The rain informs our conversations,
which are coming down with flu. Life is difficult.

In other countries they don't know this,
but lug meanings back and forth—beyond, over, or through—
the borders like luggage. As in *traduire*, from *traductio*, to move.
We move yearly, it seems; boxes of kitchen ware and books stacked in the corners.
It always rains when we move, changing our places and ourselves,
imposing on our friends.

Reading the tea leaves, the coffee grounds, Sam says:
you may expect times when you'll come to your senses in a cold, strange place
where nothing speaks your language. And here is what you do.
Take a deep breath, then ask the wind,
the birds camped near the chimney, the lilac, the gypsy moth—
but not the rain—
what they want to be called.
The eggs, the bud, the worm will answer, "We are inspired,
betrayed, traduced."

You are not to be impressed by this.
The things of this world will always complain;
there's no pleasing the things of the world.
The Port Orford cedar from which we build our ships,
the scrub jay that plants sunflower seeds so they'll sprout and be open
when the jay returns to eat them,
the wind that steals our warmth,
come between us and whatever we want to see through or within them.
And across just such gulfs, we talk on rainy days with our friends,
cold-ridden, aware of the difficulties of translation,
especially when moving.

THE OFTEN REGRETTABLE EASE WITH WHICH THINGS, THROUGH DEATH OR DISSOLUTION, ENTER THE CATEGORY OF STUFF

I have been hanging onto the title of this poem
by my fingertips for days.
From such a perch, one studies pacts of closeness:
the bushtits suspended in their soft nest, odd angles protruding—
a beak, the trace of a wing.

The crackle of opening pine cones spreads seed like wildfire.
They violate the rule of the jungle:
never let go of one vine until the next is firmly in hand.
On the other hand,
we turn things over and over in our minds like dogs settling into sleep:
tedious, vestigal moves.

Yet Spring astonishes, this year.
Wisteria drips from a neighbor's porch; morning glories, Oregon Grape,
Bewick's wren.
Fledglings leapfrog like popcorn in the underbrush.
From now on, a rule of thumb:
pure motion, scattered sound, catching things on the wing.

By the sea, we notice a sandpiper running before the tide,
like a small skiff teasing the waves.

MY DREAMS ALWAYS CONTAIN MARGINALIA

> "Books do furnish a room."
> —Anthony Powell

We begin, familiarly, in a boat
with you, your sister and father, all galoshes and Gloucester.
It's hard to tell whether we are fleeing for our lives
or pursuing a livelihood.
One end of the boat sags, unballasting the rest.
The moon's "off,"
as if painted twenty years ago and never retouched.
The clutter on board resists the light.
And the sun rises in a sore, pink sky on a world gone flat again.

We do take to the air once, heavily.
Aha, I think, *that* kind of boat,
surprised only that this decrepit specimen displays such prowess.
Islands dot the sea like braille,
though we fly low, close enough for each to be honest terrain,
if uninviting (monotone gulls and breakers).

Later, despite your sister's presence, you are about to
reveal great secrets, when,
at the crucial moment,
your father calls.
The nets must be hauled in, or a tidal wave approaches.
Maybe it's lunchtime.
I am saddened, not at what is lost,
but at being recalled.

And yet am still comforted.
I believe the islands hold the key.
After all, we live in this boat,
and shall not otherwise be transported.
Where else should we be?
No firmer terra, and from here
small translations are possible.

3. FAMILIARITY

THE TRANSLATION OF NATURAL LANGUAGES

"It is a thoughtful pupil has two thoughts
for any word."
—Marianne Moore

I can see it in the daffodils, the dogwood and the dogs:
what spring says over and over, an inventory of growth.
I say: *peonies, trillium, what-have-you.*
What the former owner of our house has left.
These appearances of someone else's life become signs of *retreat*
in the best sense of the word,
a lesser poetry of hidden losses and unearned gains.

As when my grandmother, mad collector of clippings, would stop our Sunday drives.
Face front, we'd wait. Her small figure squatting in a housedress;
with the trowel she kept in her purse, she assembled thefts from public parks.
It's a free country—
inexact, not fastened. At our feet, piles of transplanted, hairy roots.
We'd return to the house that's now long gone, not my parents' house,
by which the lilac with no mate would never bloom.

For love of the things these memories uproot, I tidy my yard,
a human interest story mild among disasters for which we have no words:
retrenchment, hunger, a friend dying in a strange city to whom I was not friend enough—
poor saint of lost causes. I give them up.
In *inventory* and *invention*, we come upon the same family,
and make it our own. The camelias are demanding this year.
I translate pure syntax, the squiggles and hooks of vine.

Dandelions, Irish jigs, the pleasantries of our days:
bouquets on the table at all times.

WINTERSCAPE REVISITED

The pilot starts us off in a flat American voice,
saying we will have free headphones
for the playin' of the music and the watchin' of the movie—
to make up for the frozen problem with the water for coffee.

When we arrive, my parents drive us past ice encased rock;
squatting down over their streams, the mills;
the staghorn sumac with its lemon smell.
This is the local color.

My mother worries about frost on the windows
while my father practices the art of the deaf
and my husband dreams of his youth:
crowds in cities, conventions where he could climb
to the twenty-seventh floor

and empty a bag of cat's eyes out the window
without getting caught.
All the way down, he watches the small pupils
past lovers, arguments, and windshields.

My mother thinks we may miss our reservation.
Near the Bulova factory, we pass a cemetery
full of those who no longer tell time anything.
We feel sorry for the silent dead
under their dirt and angels.

I have come to feel there's a slight frozen problem
with the earth.

DRAFTING A NEW LIFE

> "Do not wrangle with the heart's need."
> —George Eliot

Back in my childhood bed I try
to explain this house, a letter sent
years ago and just rediscovered. I
no longer see what I meant.
Its silence demolishes me.

To create a context for what haunts
me, my past and present swap notes,
maniacs singing in chorus. I want
them saying more than they know.
We're not to question the heart's need,

but what *does* it need? The words that history
has taken away
so we no longer know what we
lack. An absence of speech washes over the day;
trees and icicles cancel the windows.

I am posted no where, and wish I were en route.
This child, me, to whom I return
never seemed like a plausible person: I could loot
the honey with my mother's blessing, but germs
made her rule that all spoons must be clean.

My used spoon could not touch the jar. How
unending was making and making
it new. I disliked the childhood I like now.
I can see now how I thrive
raiding that sweet ignorance greedy
as a lover checking the mailbox where what's expected
will always speak more clearly
than what has arrived.

UNPREPOSSESSING EVENINGS

The sparrow on the phone wire pulses in the rain's end,
marking the voices below.
Each house on the block holds someone, wishing they'd been faithful,
but not knowing to what.
Spring always touches some nerve.

I avoid the questionnaire of the day.
What do you want and why?
A life to grow old in;
I am my father's daughter, dispossessed.
How do you grow old?
My father has the knack. I don't know.

Stories arrive to hold my doubt:
the phone sells me aluminum siding; all is well.
Grasses grow in alarming light;
flower sellers blossom on street corners.
Slickered, they glow as if possessed, hawking news.
I pore over their headlines: just another spring.

Yet I revise my life in light of these signs.
Sometimes, the birds creak into morning like hinges without doors.
In the *Iliad*, Hektor finds one birdsign best: to die for his family.
He refuses the gods, who get him anyway.
Does this mean that signs are hard to read?
Or that the world abounds with signs—

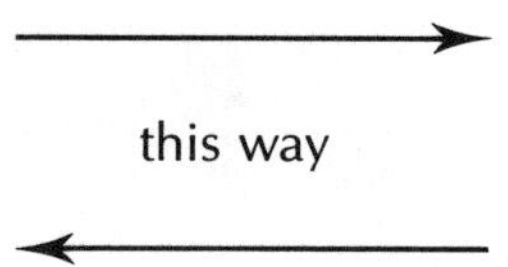

My father tells me he's stopped reading—nothing will change his life.
I introduce him to Hektor, with whom he agrees.
They're old friends.
I am surprised, and glad, and feel left out.
The birds sit dumb on the wires, which stutter with news.

GREEKS BEARING GIFTS

Reading I am too moved,
as if to have our grief so well imitated
covers our loneliness and the lessons we learn too late,
which leave us emptied, even of dreams.

I am reminded there are talismanic lines and lives:
Patroklos recalls us to the need and price of closenesses,
and comes just close enough for comfort.
Like Homer's women, we weep at his death.

I worry too that we are taken in by these creatures.
We forget we are now reading together
and apart.
These flattering images wedge between us.
Shyly, we drape them around some empty core,
as if we could not look out for each other.

Some days, lying next to you,
I imagine engulfing you that I might be alone
remembering you perfectly clasped,
our love forming an album of generations
linked like a favorite couplet quietly mouthed,
and—for a moment—enough.

POEM FOR A POLISH PROVERB

"The words will come . . ."

My grandmother in a field, caught by the woody hay,
the unseen person to whom she speaks,
silent now.

The heft of bales, once flexible grasses,
becomes part of a numbness.
Working against the threat of rain
is just what the body does, and the mind
as blank as a field after cutting.
Her history may not repeat itself,
yet has a way of rhyming.

Jewel weed still grows orange,
will turn silver under running water.
It comes cheap.
The full pods in season spring open,
disappear when touched.
And the words will come one day or later.

DOOM SOUNDS MILDLY IN THE MIDDLE DISTANCE

Last week,
a bird appeared in my house after days of rustling in the fan.
I am still surprised at the materialization & that
I accept the impossible with aplomb.

Russell says an emotion destroyed by mathematics has no value.
But I am only content when the world bends to my passes through it.
I let the bird out & it leaves.
Thoughts scuttle away, like pheasants unwilling to be flushed.
There's nothing more to be said.

I introduce Bertrand Russell to my grandparents.
They are all polite;
my grandmother tries to feed him.
The candles on the mantle, in the shape of pilgrims, sag.
The ashtray in the iron folds of a woman's evening gown is never used.
A music box piano completes their high society in miniature.
Meanwhile, Russell declines poundcake.
They are all very calm.

I am not calm.
I am seriously upset that Phyllis Schlafly has gone into government,
& look forward to the day when—
if poems are still read—
Phyllis Schlafly needs a footnote.
My lovers turn into southern belles & waltz away.
My grandfather is dying.

The world smells of hickory for no good reason.
It is also dangerous for us.
It's been raining for so long the gulls traverse the city
uncertain of what is land.
Something seems to have died.

In Trinidad, they have birds with names like gargoyles:
blue-crowned motmots,
toady flycatchers,
real lulus.
We've only gulls only feeding on the grass.

The question is how we feel about this.
The answer is:
badly
and not well.

IN THE MIDST OF, AND TALLYING

"The American language comes out of
the mouths of Polish grandmothers."
—William Carlos Williams

My grandmother's washboard and African violet basement
is upon me: the earth smell, the hollows in the stairs.
The day she died, I took my first lover—my sole acknowledgement
of loss. She lost native tongue and land.
In her country—Białstok—it must be in Polish, in kitchens, women share.
She'd been married, never mentioned her husband
not so long buried when I was born.

She would give me, from a black clasp
purse, when her check came in, nickels and dimes.
Against my father's and my mother's protests,
coins would enter my pockets on the sly.
Greedy for kitchen cabbage smells, fruit juice, time
alone with her, I knew myself the apple of her eye,
knew nothing of her heart.

I try on her first language. Krew is blood. Her three children lost
the tongue lightly. Water, for washboards, the violets that grew
in the damp; the same word even when much water has been crossed.
In an old rocking chair, she sang me songs whose wisdom I understood less
than I understood her. My violets die. Blood is not water, I read now: krew
nie water. And: old age is not happiness;
death is not bliss.

I look like my grandmother, like her have a taste
as I grow old for African violets and pineapple juice.
I could shake the coin purse, the old woman in a blue print, high-waist
apron, rolled stockings, braided fragile hair—
shaking for what might come loose.
What the living withheld, the dead will not offer:
the earth-smells of her basement hold their peace.

RELATIVITIES

I do not think I will ever grow old,
although my father does,
and my grandfather is so old he has walked off the end of the world.
My mother refuses age politely:
No, thank you, I don't believe I will.
I learn treason and tradition are doublets
and hand over my grandfather.

I collect families and facts.
At times, my cleverness betrays me.
I lust after imagination.

Strangers in the street approach me with questions.
They lust after imagination; I give them facts:
the wandering tattler summers in Alaska;
such things stick in my mind only partly for their own sake;
I give this bird a habitat that I might weather all loss.

I am talking about minds gathering what they can to ward off the worst.
Only the *idea* of my family comforts me.
Really I worry people cannot live well together.
I live alone in a city of soft water; my dentist mutters about decay;
my mouth yields intimations of mortality.

I invite garden slugs to partake of beer, salt, SNAIL AND SLUG DEATH.
The New Yorker informs me that trade first made us hold things in mind:
I am still afraid everything I love will die;
I will no longer be able to imagine myself except alone.

Woolgathering on memory and death,
I work my garden—the real, the literal peppers.
My mother and father grow old.
I cultivate hard facts, worry them to death.
It's how I keep the world and all its hungers fed,
add apples to oranges,
resist both what's easy and what is not.

FOR A FRIEND WHO LOVED WORDSWORTH

Each time, I stumble over these words—*veritas, dying*—
trying to write you a poem. And once again fail you, talking only
to the place you no longer are.

One night we argued over the sternness of love and the line,
"The good die first, my friend."
But you liked best the man who grew old
looking to his own absence and revisited hills.

Places keep offering themselves to me.
The medallion in the chapel where we gathered to mourn said *veritas*.
Veritas: those who gathered, my landscape, were beside themselves.
This landscape is not for you.

I mourn myself in those who are sad,
who return to rooms full of dishes, chairs, and empty.
They loiter on the edges of crowds, wanting to be taken home, with
nothing to say.
The aches of which they do not speak, speak for them, and we,
who have escaped for now, moving away.

I tried to side with everyone that night we argued,
for the comfort, the little we can give.
The truth is, I would change what I was more than what I'll come to.
I mourn that we do not have more time to make things right,
though things are never right.

You said the power of those lines came from what we cannot say:
there is no comfort,
but wanting it so bad, we almost come to bliss.
We keep talking for just this reason; we look up
at the chairs on the tables, and last call, and the spell is gone.

CALLING UPON THE NIGHT

My aunt, true prophet of doom, writes boring letters:
numbness of the right hand runs in the family.
Even as I speak, madmen hulking past the window
remind me of the alternatives.
I cleave to you with at least half of my whole heart.

Freud says the imagination's a capitalist.
My politics have trouble with my imagination;
I believe I can have my cake and eat it too.
In our local tavern: five motorcyclists,
including an old woman with a chain linking her leather jacket to her jeans.
She wears a wedding ring;
soft lines connect her apple cheeks with her scrawny neck.
Her laugh sets the evening on edge, and is mysterious, and,
in general, the world is not looking up.

I try to learn the densities of earth and settle down, with style.
An island in the mouth of the Columbia arrows the way: west.
The pilot tells us "there is some weather between us and Seattle,"
terrifying to think of there being none.
An announcer asks would the passenger
leaving a bag of pine cones at the Delta counter
please claim same.
I claim different things at different times:
how important it is that we break silence, like bread, together;
the way we keep each other;
whether we should or should not expect the Cossacks to arrive.
When my grandfather died, I asked him,
"Is this the Cossacks?"
He didn't answer. Is this the Cossacks?

We let language have its way with us and what do we get?
Consumer poetics. Bad company.
I wish I could say straight out:
what I want is never what I have;
the Cossacks continue to arrive.
Come with me to the Casbah.
Trust me.
It'll be awful.

About the Author

Lisa Malinowski Steinman is also the author of *Lost Poems* (Ithaca House, 1976) and of a critical study, *Made in America: Science, Technology, and American Modernist Poets* (Yale University Press, 1987). She has been awarded grants from the National Endowment for the Humanities and the National Endowment for the Arts, as well as from the Oregon Arts Commission. In addition, she has been Rockefeller Scholar-In-Residence at the 92nd Street Y Poetry Center. She lives in Portand, Oregon and teaches at Reed College.

Colophon

All That Comes to Light is set in 10 pt. Optima type. The cover art for the paper edition is taken from a monoprint, *Unrestrained,* by Chi Meredith. Fifty copies, signed and numbered by the author, have been bound into boards.
